Then She Kissed El Paco's Lips Now! Or April in DeKalb

Poems

Ricardo Mario Amézquita

Indian Paintbrush Poets
Colorado

Copyright © 2012 Ricardo Mario Amézquita. All rights reserved.

I would like to thank my fellow poets and friends John Bradley, Jana Brubaker, Rex Burwell, Joe and Jean Gastiger, Christine Holloway, Tony Kallas, John and Peggy Knoepfle, Craig McGrath, Becky Parfitt, Susan Porterfield, and my wife, Bonnie, for their editorial advice and support.

Acknowledgements:

A number of the poems in this collection have been published previously in *The Alchemist Review, Eating Stones, CARACOL, Discourse: Journal for Theoretical Studies in Media and Culture, Kalligraphia, Many Smokes, Ping-go, Poetry &, Poets Against the War, The Rockford Review, Rosie: Selected Works by Rosie Richmond*, and *The Spoon River Quarterly*.

Cover design and interior by Paperwork

Indian Paintbrush Poets is an imprint of
Pearn and Associates, Inc., Book Publishing
1600 Edora Court Suite D
Fort Collins, Colorado 80525
http://pearnandassociates.wordpress.com/
For manuscript submission query by mail,
or email victorpearn@ymail.com.

Library of Congress Control Number: 2012942364

Amézquita, Ricardo Mario
Rezo Resbaloso, by Ricardo Mario Amézquita
ISBN 978-0-9846523-8-9 paperback

Printed in the United States of America
Canada, United Kingdom, Europe and Australia

1st edition.

For John Knoepfle, poet, mentor, friend

Noctambulous

Solid ground　　　　floating on sea
not lost　　　　　　iceberg belief
isolated　　　　　　suspended
to reoccur　　　　　cyclic amnesia
from myself　　　　in vacuum
the picture of a flame/ reaching home
　　a poem i never read

Contents

Rotten Grapes and Other Miracles — 1

Absent Without Leave — 2
Working for CETA — 3
Hangover Poem No. 3 — 5
Horror No. 4 — 6
Main Street Near the Barrio — 7
Y Yo Soy Un Borracho Sin Botella — 8
To Chihuahua, Chihuahua — 9
Ping-go — 10
Scratching A Scab — 11
Rotten Grapes and Other Miracles — 12

Being — 13

Song of Uroborus — 14
Emmenagogue — 15
The turtle — 16
Dust-devil — 17
Hand Harvest — 18
Crow — 19
Son And Father — 20
Madbirth — 21
Eating Stones — 22
July 8, 1996 — 23
Untitled — 24
Being — 25

Faith as a Third Eye 27
Poetry Heels: Conflict of Interest 28
Frau Monroe? 29
Blue Winter 30
For Ken Saro-Wiwa 31
The Smell of Gossip 32
Faith as a Third Eye 33

We Are What We Bomb 35
We Are What We Bomb 36
Kokura: City Spared 37
Winter in the Barracks 38
Star Date 299-56* 39
Call to War 40
W's WW 41
Contributions on the Day of the Dead 43

Para Rosita: Speedball Melancholia 45
Asphyxia: The Lover 46
To Rosie 47
Midnight Walk 48
You Say You Did Not Sleep Well 49
Saturday Morning 50
For Rosie: From the Dream Journal (2-6-94)
    While Thinking of You 51
For Rosie: From the Dream Journal (2-8-94)
    Honey, Your Angel Is Here 52
For Rosie: From the Dream Journal (2-21-94) 53
Rush 53
Avocado Gone 54
Because the Door Is Open 55
¿Que Pasa Con El Sol? 57

2 AM	59

From: Where Miracles Happen

Buffeting Blues	60
Para Rosita: Speedball Melancholia, Or What Are Flowers For?	61

Dynamics for Collision — 63

Title (Pick One)*	64
Jesus' Last Thoughts (Good Friday, 4/5/96)	65
Cobwebs in the Confessional	67
Getting into Heaven By the Back Door, But Not Staying Very Long	68
October 31st	70
Two Dreams	71
Dance of Xilonen	72
Dynamics For Collision	73

Reversing Gravity: Sha-Boom Sha-Boom — 75

Reversing Gravity—Sha-Boom Sha-Boom	76
Dedicated to Elvis: Mas Cubano Que Rey	77
Milagro, pues	79
3 Spiders	81
Red Miata	82
Tiburón	83
Glacier	84
nocturne	85
Samba de Orfeu	86
Turkey Explodes	87

Then She Kissed El Paco's Lips Now! Or April in DeKalb — 89

The Dreamer	90
Dimension of Poem	91
Then She Kissed El Paco's Lips Now! Or April in DeKalb	92
Perhaps	93

Direk Tutmak   94
You Heard a Robin!   95

Epilogue
Rezo Resbaloso: Slippery Prayer or Prayer While Sliding   97
Rezo Resbaloso   98

Author's Notes   101

Rotten Grapes and Other Miracles

Absent Without Leave

I walked beneath the Rotunda
its seams fissured in my mind.

The girl at the Information Desk asked,
    "May I help you?"
      "Yes," I said.
        "I have lost my memory.
       It is pale
          and has a handle that is
          hard to hold on to."

Working for CETA

Once a week, each Monday morning, a counselor is sent to the satellite office at the Adult Center. The voc. counselor is seated at his desk with *selected poetry* by Richard García and slowly savoring a homemade tamale. He occasionally glances at his multi-colored Aztec calendars shirt making sure no chili has escaped his fingers.

Enters Mrs. Su Fung, ESL instructor.

MSF: Help Sam! Help Mohammad! They need work!

Juan: Try the classified ads and the Employment Office.

MSF: Oh they can't—they don't have a green card.

Juan: Yes, I know. They told me they didn't have a work-permit.

MSF: The Employment Office will not service them without green card. It takes too long to get one. Even after I graduated from USC it took me two years to get one. And I'm married to an American.

Juan: They can still work at some unskilled job. Like busboy, dishwasher.

MSF: You don't know the trouble it is to get a green card!

Juan: ¿Como un nopal?

MSF: What?

Juan: I was born here but I have heard about the problem.

MSF: Perhaps you could take them to some restaurants and help them get a job.

Working for CETA

Juan: I'm sorry but that's not my job. I am not a placement service. I can only tell them where to look for a job and I've done that. Besides, I can't speak Arabic so you see I really wouldn't be much of a translator.

MSF: OK. Thank you.

Juan: Sure

Hangover Poem No. 3

All this
fucking money, four dollars
and 12 cents
"eat your olives
speedy gonzales"
ay qué frijoles de saber
tienes

I tell the truth
and you treat me with
violence
o josé i feel so sick
last rites for radicals
thank you

And beloved david
can't be found
and i must add
my hours for mister small

Granada mojada waved
thru the window
at the blue upholstery
to myself, yes
it feels like it

This morning i brushed
three teeth 'til my
gum bled

Horror No. 4

Only now the
vice-president said hello
to his cigar and passed
by my sleeping kneecap

His blurring checkered
suit remains in a glance
stored near my ribs.

I take a spider from my hair
to let it roam
the pink sheet I scribble on
he hides in the
hole at the edge

Main Street Near the Barrio

Seeing new fall styles
   I know the colors I will wear next winter
Red-stocking ladies are Christmas shopping
   Solo tomó una cerveza
Hoy esta mojado sin novedad
   Today is wet without novelty.

Y Yo Soy Un Borracho Sin Botella

Go away rufus
your eye is closed
i'm not cold
your picture is what i want to see

You fail as a psychotic
and still you may be
a writer
poets never write
they don't know how.

Dogs and children
bothersome company
one licks my salt
one opens my wound

Unknown is everywhere
fleas catch breath
my pride stands
without friends

To Chihuahua, Chihuahua

He says
he likes
to wear keys on his belt
because the jingling
reminds him of spurs
and a dusty trail
grandfathers rode

Ping-go

Y José habló primero,

> "This used to be a German prisoner of war camp
> but now it's the Joan of Arc farm headquarters
Same chain link fence topped off with barbed wire."

The shacks smudged with twilight huddle the sleeping hands.

José habló otra vez,

> "I bet them farmers didn't like last night's
> rain. Que sean pobres como nosotros."

Me siento como un limón de la barra.
Yo soy una cabeza de lechuga que ha estado debajo del sol por tres días.

We migrants hold the day between our toes.

Scratching A Scab

I picket for justice
Do not tell me to go home
My history is my face

I eat frijoles
You share my land
But I am not your neighbor

Rotten Grapes and Other Miracles

    Where blackeagle soars
    A red crest leads the tide
        Huelga is in the ear

Leaf-pullers are now tugging lobes,
    "Come out of there, countrymen,"
    shouts a Filipino striker.

    While scabs prune grapevines
We pay for fruit never picked.

Being

Song of Uroborus

the bones
the bones
the bones
are buried there
are buried there
are buried here
the bones are buried
they are cold
they sweat
they wait
the bones
the bones

Emmenagogue

    Behind groundsel tree
            rhinoceros' horn lifts
the carbuncular moon

The turtle

          following concrete lines
thinks of
cool mud
and a river song.

Dust-devil

Today i am

a dust-devil
searching for

a scorpion

to play with.

Hand Harvest

we
      grind corn
             eat tortillas
                    and
                          comb our children's hair

Crow

Crow father your children have been taken
Crow mother searching in the cornfields
Crow brother the woods are shaking
Crow sister flying over the river
Crow children listening . . .
                The robin gives you worms.

Son And Father

Horizon
on blade of grass
a drop reflecting
another breed

Madbirth

    a frustrated child
       struggles putting
      his head into
                  the skull

Eating Stones

Little brother
Little brother
                You ate some bennies
                        you thought them
            candy
Now you run around like a motorcycle
                              in a pit
I hide in the white house   waiting . . .
I don't think I can write your   eulogy.

July 8, 1996

Papá,

All day whenever I wrote the date I thought, "It is your cumpleaños. You would have been ochenta today." Is this my desire for you to hear my good-bye?

Is this why in a dream abuelita visited me, tearing the bathroom linoleum as she emerged from the sótano? You know she just died this past December 3. Frightened, I just stood there as a ten-year-old in two pair of calzones no longer thinking of the plugless clay drain in this first casa you bought, Papá. This first casa I lived in and this last casa abuelita owned where she could live free.

Abuelita, you unlock the bathroom door and tell me not to watch the magic mirror as you point to the medicine cabinet. "Look at the visions on the wall. Two on each side of the mirror." I only see luminous lines. I turn but abuelita's gone.

I take off a pair of jockey shorts and start the bath. Water too cool, but el baño isn't filling. I discover no metal in the chain of the rubber stopper I manage to wedge into the chipped drain. The chips and smell of wet clay remind me of abuelo's hand-painted Mexican mug on his night mesita, the coolness of water, and the darkness of earth. The bathwater becomes ocean blue. I remove my second pair of shorts.

You return, abuelita, to wash clothes in the old ringing-wringer machine and to tell me that my brother must also change his ways, not carry such a load. Change directions.

Pienso de las líneas luminosas y oigo el oleaje del mar.

Untitled

When bearded giant
swings ax to Tree
and thunder shakes forest
my sister and I
run mile away
huddle by rock

Trunk cracks
giant howls
slips and gnarls foot
as Tree slowly falls
crushes ribs, deafens
hurtles stones and snow to sky

We embrace
branches plummet
piercing once each forehead
stabbing both in one eye
breath frozen
we listen for birds.

Being

      Ax to our bellies
           we become
                  fallen chips
                        a page of
                                firelight

Faith as a Third Eye

Poetry Heels:
Conflict of Interest

Where are the poems that
    spit lead
        carve knuckles and shatter
       the brittle tongue?
... poems that rape your hypocrisy
behind a fireplace and dehumanize
your breath with antiseptic
shoe polish?

      "pitch pennies/ roll a rook
       mate your mate/ stab a book,"

where crocodiles on 79th street
wait for mushrooms in blackened bottles.
They are urinating the mountain
faces
    holy plaster of mary falls onto
a fetus before fatmen's
testicles are roasted over
the bones of our brothers
because forcause tocause
pieces of war shooting blood
smack and movies for
zenith junkies
who cannot tell a lie.

Frau Monroe?

Marilyn
when was your icon bought by the Fourth Reich?
On back of TIME in doctor's office
I saw the Mercedes-Benz ® circle
where your beauty mark used to be

Who sold your beauty?
Why was I not told?

Do the chants of "it doesn't matter" awaken them
twice a night?
How did I discover Mars on my footsteps this morning?

Tell me
Tell me before throttled clouds
swallow yellow butterflies.

Blue Winter

My dream must've flown in from some tundra.

—I was trapped behind the mirror looking at myself,
Studying in a restaurant, standing up, walking towards the cashier
    with my books. What was I studying for?

People standing around, giving me space—and why not? I was
about a foot taller—but that wasn't strange.

My reflection was strange. I was wearing the uniform of an Illinois
State Trooper, and I was studying for a test at the NCO
    academy.

Now I remember. My father had been so proud. He swore me in, if
    that's what you call it.

The last time I was this clean and cut was 1966, basic training.
    (That was another time, and some say another war.)

I wonder if I really like my father. Or was it a matter of pleasing?

Should one ever please authority? Or love pleasing?

For Ken Saro-Wiwa

Nigeria
    today I saw you standing on the corner
    of Park Avenue and Lincoln Highway
    crying under Anglo-Dutch symbol
    flaunting WORLD'S BEST SELLING GASOLINE
    like some frozen flamethrower
    claiming red blood for black
Nigeria
    why are you staring at the patrons
    nozzling their gas tanks
    ignoring the flapping of clothes
    that wind can not steal?
    America buys half
    of your black gold
    while STRONGLY CONDEMNING
    the general's regime
    for executing nine Ogoni sons
    who complained of spillage
    and had audacity to ask for
    a share of revenues
    from their tribal land.
Nigeria
    why not stand in hot smog
    of flaring tongues
    so close to the sea?
    What SHALL we do
    now that the fashion show
    is over
    and QUIET DIPLOMACY
    has failed?

The Smell of Gossip

Saturday morning.
The assembly begins.
Four groups meet
in three rooms
while many stand in the hallway
wearing winter coats.

I am pressed in a collection of overaged
housewives, retired husbands,
bipolar cab drivers, psychogenic scribes,
and seventeen-year under-the-ground cicadas.
A derelict corps that cannot hold.
No familiar face in sight.

The smell of gossip and smoke
is thicker than earwax.
Where in the Cosmos are you, Christ?
Have you fallen down with your crosspiece
among the Gypsies? We've heard the lamentations
driving past llama farms. Buddha, we need you,
and Martin, too! They have taken away
our black plums our mayapples.
Our diet is betel nuts and lime.
Have you forsaken us?

But lo and behold,
there in transparent cubicle,
the leonine messenger,
the salt and pepper prince,
the Twentieth Century Archetype of Urban Miracles,
former Chicago Bulls coach,
Mr. Phil Jackson.

He uncrosses his arms and motions me over
to the booth. After brief salutations he asks me,

> *How would you like to thrust a dirk*
> *into the stoneheart of Amerika?*
> *There'll be three grand in it for you*
> *at the end of the show.*
> *Here's my card and studio address.*
> *We'll be doing a satellite hookup.*

Faith as a Third Eye

driving blind this morning
first through fog
then sun
I could not help but think
that you, Death, rode
past me last night
as I hurried from
the garage
clutching briefcase
and coffee cup

my right ear
told me to turn around
your body looked
so at peace
relaxed
riding your bike
with a slight meander
the only bright spot
a front reflector
no, I did not see your face
in that pale hood

I could not think or say
"good evening"
how could i
in a world so in love
with you?

We Are What We Bomb

We Are What We Bomb

I'm walking towards my bird
the crew chief who resembles
Peter Lorre hands me my chute
and whispers a rumor:

There's been a bomb threat.
K-nines didn't find
anything. Be careful, sir.
The enemy is everywhere.

I climb into the B-24 Liberator
hold my breath, start engines,
release brakes, and salute
waving crew chief below.

Taxiing in reverse, I squint
at twilight, hoping to miss
other craft and buildings.
I find runway's end.

~ ~ ~

Bomb bays open
I'm hit with flak*
my console becomes
a light-show of warnings and failures.

I am the pilot, co-pilot, navigator,
nose, dorsal, waist, tail, ball turret-gunner
and now bombardier over bombsight.
Attack run begins.

Releasing over the orphanage
gifts, candy, food, and clothes
Olé Piñata begins losing altitude.
I don my chute and pray to make the coast.

*fliegerabwehrkanonen: flyer + defense + cannons

Kokura: City Spared

Partly cloudy
three times rising sun
not dropped
Pluto's anvil finds your neighbor
leaves the nimbus that you respect

Does relief join sorrow?
Some say handkerchief
invented to conceal lack
of tears at funerals
but men are not supposed to cry

As a child i lost playground battle
arrived home crying
was punished
called a *travieso y buscaplietos**
i did not know the rules

A year since my grandfather's death
i caught a bass never knowing
when hook set
killed asphyxiating fish then
tears grandfather tears

naughty and troublemaker

Winter in the Barracks

It is cold
we borrow blankets from the
unassigned bunks
snow enters through cracked windows
and crevices in the ceiling

I dream of a summer night at home
in the kitchen drinking beer and
the longest conversation I ever had
with my father. I wake up and know
it is not true. There are no crickets.

Star Date 299-56*

Star date 299-56, 5:00AM:
A new war

Even before the WTC twins fell
Prophets had warned us
Now what can we do?

Dios mio . . .

Shall I teach *The War Myth*?
Shake the dust off my draft avoidance manual?
Fly the flag upside down?

I worry for my students
Have they forgotten to come back to school?
They have fallen behind
Will they return soon?

His brother died
In aircraft that hit our war center
Her friend gone
In Trade Center fire

¡Ojalá!

Washing my hands after touching
U. S. mail, I wonder,
What are authorities doing
To my map of Afghanistan?

299: Number of days lived so far this year
56: Number of years since the bombing of Hiroshima

Call to War

Comes the final Lie
Words
Like summer tar on asphalt

Blood black as oil

W's WW

Fear sits on the lip of my coffee mug. My panic attack subsides as anxiety is exhaled. What would I have done? Can the word "God" be a prayer?

• • • •

Leaving for my early morning shift, I witnessed a double dose of a fiery sky, a heavy curtain slowly rising to reveal a translucent veil and a glow. There appeared to be a nightlight just below the horizon. The sky was becoming aqua but still navy blue velvet above with bright stars. I almost wondered if the moon was below the horizon until I saw pink and orange on the clouds. The harvested fields were covered with a low mist or fog that gave the illusion of a white desert. Suddenly, the sky was afire and I was horrified. The colors and configuration of the clouds made for a scene from the Ultimate Doomsday Weapon: A Thermonuclear Detonation. On the radio someone was being interviewed, talking of Vera Lynn's movie career and the song, "We'll Meet Again." Then, they played it.

Blinded by the sun, I thought, Chicago is gone. How long before the blast breaks my windshield if I don't duck'n cover now? And even if I do find cover and manage to escape the wrath of debris, how long before the oxygen in my lungs is consumed, vaporized, my skin blistered, burned, and/or melted. How long before I become one with the bomb? Why can't I wake up?

I make it to work on time.

• • • •

That night I dream
the phone rings.
The airbase summons me to report.
Code Red:0900 Zulu
The nightlight is out: No power.
I stumble to find flashlight, then flight suit
I'm ordered to aircraft A-3409/ Line 26
I'm the Life Support System Specialist
for a B-52.

Should I stop at
the KFC
pick up
a dozen plus
boxes for the crew?
Tell Jose
all bets are off!
Why do you have to go, my wife says.
It's my duty.
Why else, I think.
Then I say, I'd rather be here with you
if it's the end.
I hold her tight,
close my eyes
and I awake.

Contributions on the Day of the Dead

While you dine for dollars
your henchmen
stalk quiet wakes
for coins that rest on eyes
of fallen soldiers.

You will have them render
unto Caesar
what is yours.

You massage with thumb
the widow's mite
ponder your next
pre-emptive Terror for terror
strategy.

Are you afraid to look
into the eyes
beneath the coins?

That may explain your absence
at funerals.

You might see your own death
in theirs.

Para Rosita:
Speedball Melancholia

Asphyxia: The Lover

Your lips
awaken me
like a rush of doves
I,
the hummingbird,
plant one hundred kisses
on petals
    devour nectar
and become
iridescence

To Rosie

The first time I remember focusing on Rosie was the summer of '76 at Sangamon State in Lit. 480: Modern Poetry. It was T.S. Eliot, Rilke, and "William Buttereggs" as she said her young son, Al, would pronounce it. Nose in her book, wearing straw hat, blouse, floral skirt, and sandals, poised and posh, she must have recently migrated from some section of San Francisco. Were you as studious in your poetry lesson as I was of you? ... No surface or medium. What could Picasso, Renoir, or Monet have done? ...

What made me fall in love with her though I didn't know it then? It was the day we gathered at the cafeteria for refreshments and reflections on the morning lecture. I can not speak for the camaraderie, but I was surely hooked by her humorous tale of the uninvited (?) big fish that came to dinner in a wagon pulled by alley kids. Her timing and unassuming charm has kept me laughing inside and out....

I'll never forget our first "date" if that is the proper word. Didn't know drinking a few beers and praying could yield such results. I asked or wished for an angel and five minutes later I was giving Rosie (a.k.a. Angel, she told me later) a ride home. Don't know how I managed a kiss that evening. Perhaps, I was hit by a meteor, a confluence of strawberry daiquiris, coincidental tunes from cross-time musicians, summer heat and nightclub cool. *Metanoia* comes from rose petals and kissing them primal joy incarnate: *satori* ....

Midnight Walk

Midnight walk
Under lightning
You open a door
And i become
The breeze

You Say You Did Not Sleep Well

Under cobalt flashes
I stumbled over
brass skulls
into a basement corner
away from the green woman
who is now addressing
shadows and spirits
my hands reflex in darkness
absent—your left shoulder
absent—your left breast
I pray for
the warm caress of your fingers
subduing my desire
while your tongue
      a poniard
           savoring
                color
                      & death

opens the knot
that will echo
t/h/r/o/u/g/h/t/h/e/r/a/i/n

Saturday Morning

As I enter the garage
A great wolf attacks me
I shove my fist into its throat
Grab its nape to choke it more

Scared and angry I wake up
With a knot in my stomach
Wondering why I am cold
And alone in your warm bed

Remembering today is your surgery
The surgery that will remove
Cancer from your colon
And anywhere else they can

Like a race against the night
Where the purse is precious
We hope for Hope to place or show
Fabricating the odds that never win

On the coldest day of the year
I growl because of tearless ducts
Scowl with succor less arms for you
Knowing tomorrow will be colder still

For Rosie: From the Dream Journal (2-6-94) While Thinking of You

Wake up at 6 AM
take two cold tablets
a drink of water
go back to bed

I close my eyes
while thinking of you
and nod-off

I see a woman's torso
vibrating colors
the head and members engulfed
by bright light

Turning away from the brilliance
I see an eye as big as
my field of vision
very fluorescent and pulsing

Is this dream vision or hallucination?
I think, "How can the morning sun
be shining through the west window?"
And I forgot to close the curtain

I open my eyes
to closed curtains
and cloudy day

I call your friend so not to disturb you
she tells me last night was the first time
you slept all night in weeks
Me too, I say

For Rosie: From the Dream Journal (2-8-94)
Honey, Your Angel Is Here

We're in an apartment like yours
only narrower
I'm in the bedroom
when a black woman enters unexpectedly
she wants to see you
I tell her you're not here
I know you're taking a bath
I want to know her identity
I don't want to take her to you
I tell her she reminds me of a pop singer
I thought dead
I ask her about the Ronettes Chiffons Crystals Shirelles
Ruby & the Romantics Nancy Wilson's Long White
Room
the death of Mary Wells You Beat Me to the Punch
What's Easy for Two is Hard for One
the Beatles' version of He's So Fine
the future of the Temptations
Frank Zappa Muddy Waters Albert Collins
I'm looking around the room
notice a black and white photo of you
Have you ever heard this Angel CD?
Rosie and the Originals start belting Angel Baby
running out of questions
I want to find a phone
call you *"Do you know a _____?"*
look at this silent woman for a response a name
"She wants to see you. Is that ok?"
She is beautiful smiling Heraldo Negro
the Penguins are now singing Earth Angel

For Rosie: From the Dream Journal (2-21-94)

I am massaging your feet
for the last time
remembering
how you love them
to be rubbed
preferring this over food
cigarettes or a mystery
you'd moan cry
please don't stop
sometimes you'd compare this
to dying and going to paradise
I think you invented the adage
you remind me of my commitment
as I begin the last phase of the massage
My hands are your shoes for life
you say I said
on wine-loosened tongue
our longest night
I look at your white feet
between your toes tears streaming
with thin red rivulets
the drops near your ankle
blush like zinfandel

Rush

Tonight
numb with pain
numb with fatigue
and now numb with
cold
what use living:
to hear the robin sing
on snowy branch

Avocado Gone

The candle has gone out

My spirit huddles in a
corner under a quilt

Bitten by seasons
i go to the bathroom
and shake like a dog

Because the Door Is Open

I

1968
NEWSWORTHY EVENTS IN THE WORLD TODAY:
GIRL FOUND ALIVE FOLLOWING FUNERAL
KARACHI, Pakistan (AP)_____
After the funeral of a 2 ½ year old
her mother dreamed
an old man dressed in white told her,
"Go and dig the grave and
you will find your child alive."
Telling her dream to neighbors
she insisted on reopening the grave
and a large crowd found the child alive
sucking her thumb sitting in the coffin
50 hours after buried for dead.
Recovering at home in Liaquatabad
the "miracle child" has been visited by thousands.

II

Was this the news account
that caused me to dream of you?
the imbedded <u>*"a miracle waiting message"*</u>
of the speaker in the dream of the dreamer?
Was it just the word, "*miracle*"?
Like the name given to the female white buffalo calf
born on your birthday the year you died?
Great hopes for the Sioux and all nations
A warning to live with the earth or perish.
Or was it the five cups of decaffeinated Earl Grey
a Christmas gift from my niece
that I drank while watching the last half of
<u>*The Fall of the Roman Empire*</u> till 3AM and thinking

Para Rosita: Speedball Melancholia

Sophia Loren is still beautiful?
Was it the desire to want you tonight next to me
and your form constructed with three pillows
with only your mask missing?
Or was it eventually sleeping in the middle
of the bed instead of the left side?
Is this what evoked you to be in my dream?
What Kabbalah did I stumble onto?

III

Morning half-light
swarms of bees silent
like leaves turning wings
to flocks

Each wood-swallow hawking
swarm to swarm against
arterialized sky
fork-tails returning to wood and note

Swarms attack neighbors' son
on second floor who now can not
install storm window
I enter house to help

Find you there
"You died last week," I say not understanding
You tell me *be patient and wait in the bedroom*
We bathe together and make love for a minute

Because the door is open.
"No one told me
How did you do it?
How did you come back?"

¿Que Pasa Con El Sol?

What's wrong with the sun?
Approaching aphelion
a total solar eclipse
but no outer corona
to be taken
as the umbra diagonally
crosses Illinois
dropping air temperature
ten degrees by Lake Michigan

In plum tree
birds' songs change
naked eyes warned
not for another ninety-six years

This is not the problem
nor observance of shadow column
like javelin foreboding
my destination
jet trail phenomenon
proves wrong
luck of free tickets food beer
cubs beat giants
though we leave before the last
three outs

¿Que Pasa Con El Sol?

No
it is the intense heat
tanning through
torn jeans
cooking my eyeballs
like no eggs frying
on jet wings of august
luke air force base
1967 corn oil g.i.

Is it true
what they said on the radio?
ozone layer going
skin cancer rates up
sheep in argentina
blinded by the sun
last year

memory's mirage
echoes
where's your hat
grass sunbather

I can't cry anymore
then do.

2 AM

Strange late movie; stranger title. Old Red never knew the truth but died finding the evidence. The obsession was clocks, "a day's work for a night's sleep," and sometimes snow. Not *The Ticking Man*. What's left, Mr. Romantic? Denial at the expense of death? Fearless against the Caster of Shadows, Love shall feel no cold. The citizens of Harper will come after you. It's closing in. Escape and you fall; fall and you die. Pleasant dreams.

From: Where Miracles Happen
Buffeting Blues

Hanging clothes on the line, I told her it was regulated
       madness soothed by an intermittent current of pain,
       various pains, an overwhelming of soul and mind
       while the heart braces for another test measuring
       hardness by calculating hydraulic steel ball. The curve
       of imagination cannot escape either.
       I'm a broken dragonfly swimming in muddy eddy. There is
       no hope, just instinct.

Para Rosita: Speedball Melancholia
Or What are Flowers For?

A most peculiar town
where the difficult dead
lie beside the road against trees
and on a curb
no cars or trucks in this town
just youngsters on scooters made from lawn mowers
Here toilet tanks are waterbeds with white goldfish

On my way out of town
I stop at the Sunrise Café
you are sitting in a booth
I join you
you grasp my index finger
I didn't expect you   I want to say
What made you appear?
Was I talking too much about you?
Speaking your words?

You show me an advertisement
and lift the words and numbers off the flyer
        Blues Concert-City Park-St Louis-7:33 to 11:29
You say you're going
I can't I have to prepare my lesson on standard time

Para Rosita: Speedball Melancholia Or What are Flowers For?

A man invites you to his booth
I guess it's time for me to go
How do I say *Adiós* ?
Shall I say it to your face
with this Johnny-standing-by
or excuse myself
head for the restroom and
have the waitress give you my note:
¿Para qué son las flores?
        ¿Para qué son las flores?

Dynamics for Collision

Title (Pick One)*:

      1) Bowling For Collards
      2) A Human Concept
      3) Oh! It Must Be A Beer-Frame Dear

Story: How to get to God? Every Monday night He is in the center of a molecule which is the dynamics of a bowling alley. You ask Him, "God, is this Heaven?"
"Shhh! Don't interrrupt, this is a beer frame."

*This has been a story-poem.

Jesus' Last Thoughts
(Good Friday, 4/5/96)

my remembrance: a moment
the world passed through me
or I through it
here in this hallway
looking at you
your lips moving
but no sound

critical mass reached by a word
perhaps a forgotten gesture too
something primordial in the psyche
like the first pictured pyramid
the first enchilada tasted
hyperspace discovered

your day nap
my night sleep

we exchange dreams:
lightning controlled
by finger on your chin
waiting for directions
Are you the antagonist
in a Hitchcock film
contemplating your demise?
Your Annie Oakley digit
has never missed in daylight.

Jesus' Last Thoughts (Good Friday, 4/5/96)

My version:
I tell you I aim at that
stupid architect's toaster
from my car behind two
elderly women in big
white caddy
but miss the brick's roof
and lightning hits between stop sign
and tree.
Our cars won't
start temporarily
but do after several tries.

We wonder on
horse hair mattress

I am left with amnesia
no place to point
neither relic nor artifact

Cobwebs in the Confessional

where are they

priest says mass in a backroom
till the wine is consumed

where are they

the Eucharist has no tongue
the "gilded hearse" corrodes

where are they

aphids cling — the rose hangs
black and white elms remain in ashes

Getting Into Heaven By the Back Door, But Not Staying Long

I was leaving the office
early today (for some reason)
and started to sing in Latin
while descending the flights of stairs.

Passing through the exit door
I enter a cathedral's anterior.

There are, perhaps, two dozen
men on both sides of the font
near the entrance.

Their costumes suggest the Orient.
I approach them and notice
the elegance
of their apparel. I behold the precious
stones on their hands and chains.
They wear headdresses with jewels
or crowns of green-gold. Most have
beards. Many are of dark complexion.

They stand waiting, silent. A man appears
garbed in a long navy-blue robe
embroidered and embellished with gold.
He wears wire-rimmed glasses and a white skull
cap. The men surround him. They are smiling
and hugging this man. He is John Paul the First.

I leave the cathedral through
the same exit door.
I am outside of the main
cathedral entrance. Beside me
is a young man with a red beard
dressed in white.

He asks me, "Why do Mexicans commit
suicide to cover the Pope's feet?"

I tell him, "Maybe they ran out of
cockroaches," and shrug my shoulders.

He accompanies me to the curb and
bids me farewell.

The road from town is covered with ice—
in the glazed sheet a marble-size hole
contains a wasp. I walk to the shoulder and
return with a leaf. Using the stem, I turn
the wasp on its stomach, then continue my
journey. The recesses with wasps grow numerous.
I ignore their frozen stares.

A fog bank lies past the timber line.
The road is now snow packed. I find
a newspaper clipping on the ground.
It reads:
>*"Few things are harder to put up with*
>*than the annoyance of a good example."*
>—Pudd'nhead Wilson's Calendar
>Mark Twain

October 31ST

Across the street
church walls echo
scraping shovels

stained glass patterns light

outside I read from
right to left and
translate "In Memory Of..."

the Master watches
as I turn all
parking meters into
aspergilla and bless
the uniforms of school children

Two Dreams

In outer space descending quickly
an entity alongside me
communicates telepathically.

It says, "Observe the polar cap.
Measure the distance from that glacier
before you and the sea below.
The ice sheet rises slowly."

Under ice a larger black-lava cap
with bright orange crevices
pushes the glacier.
The explanation is simple.

I notice the entity's twin
high above us in black space.
Their shapes tan and white
piebald, headless, and leg-less moths.

At speed fantastic
yet motionless they flash
like cards into a worm-hole.
They tell me others are watching.

Dance
of
Xilonen

I hold
the smoking mirror
to your face
the dancers
will come forth
for a moment
you will see
all being
earth roots
and the spring
where your soul
is born.

Dynamics For Collision

"... substance is between matter."

thus god   thus creativity
the actual movement   )energy(
the living force
thermal wings of friction
vibrate the senses into
relative dreams into
random death
returning to the sun
becoming green
under waves

Reversing Gravity: Sha:boom Sha:boom

Reversing Gravity — Sha:boom Sha:boom

Rumor is, not since the collapse of star No. 39
In Quasar 0241 + 622 has the science officer been
The same; although he still believes that comets
Are the original transports of life. He is present-
Ly undergoing pain-modulation therapy.

Dedicated to Elvis:
Mas Cubano Que Rey

Laughed
and called me mean
when i told them His
knee had moved
warned them
   don't open it
as i stared at the glass-encased
                                     cuerpo
looking mas cubano que Rey
stitched your upper lip
to make you smile   embalmer loco
walking up stairs
at the top cuando
petrifying gritos ignite
again y otra vez   luego
    tore her head off! tore her head off!
that is what the dead do after they have awakened
my waiting amigo y yo stumble and run
into la calle   oncoming car swerves
screeches 4wheel drift with an angry fist
but no fight
we jump into rube-machine
y a la colon   two runaway turistas
in the backseat
on the camino again
in the rearview mirror two caras drained
whiter than the Rey's vegas traje
tres horas later we stop for gas

Dedicated to Elvis: Mas Cubano Que Rey

    water and food to go
    los turistas aficionados standing
    by my black chevy shaking
    how can i tell them   end of the road, amigos
    they gave all of their dinero
    i lean through the window
    turn el radio on y
        love me tender love me true
    they run down the interstate
    ojalá some trooper stops them
    before they go muy far

    woke up last night
    leg calambre
    never did stop in vegas.

Milagro, pues...

Remote visualization.

Used it to keep sharks away from the raft,
tapping some source,
not sure how it works.

Seeing things before seeing them,
the rescue-helicopter faltering
becomes a butterfly
till the seashore is beneath us.

Today I search.
Space to park for a short time
is my desire and
I try to see it,
but a black pickup (no flashers on)
parked in the **fifteen minutes
user must use flashers spot**
keeps me from my errand
and there is no meter waiting
for this Decal-less citizen.

I go to the local café,
stare at the Hawaiian shirt
of a customer whose sex I can't determine,
drink my Guatemalan coffees,
eat toasted french-roll with cucumber-dill
cream-cheese
and read the bad news on Pine Ridge res.

Milagro, pues...

An hour later I return.
Pickup still there.
I drive around while
seeing this truck towed.
I park behind it.

I'm going to write the plate number down,
report it to the Parking Division
and suggest it be towed immediately.
I almost laugh.

As I'm reaching for my pen,
a man with a tool bag slung
over his shoulder opens the pickup's door.
I power window down
and ask, "Are you leaving?"
"Yes," he says,
crumpling the tickets off his windshield.

Voilà!

3 Spiders

#1
Why are you hiding
in that translucent pink
bottle of crème-rinse
by the basement shower?

Are you sleeping?
Is it forever?
Or just intoxicated
dreaming of perfumed hair?

#2
Under stairs a bubble
encases the spider.
Your legs half the length of
my arms.

Top pair are metallic and scooped.
Your third pair are fork-lifts.
In your mania you
fail to see me waving.

#3
In this corner weighing less than
ten drops of water is Daddy Long Legs.
So easy to spot against white walls
and ceiling.

Haven't heard of me?
I'm the heavyweight spider-killer of the world!
Five or six on a good day, but please tell me
more trapeze stories

before you die

Red Miata

In passenger seat
Japanese woman
waves me over
smiling shows
her lack of
undergarments
asks me to
drive her
home

Raising my eyebrows I offer
my regrets and continue searching
for my former Korean student
to ask her the meaning
and uses of the five
sauce bowls

Tiburón

                                    I
                             paddle
                    in blue lagoon
               come upon sleeping
          shark on curved palm tree.
        He is six feet long, gray with a
      man's head. His face olive-colored
    with a bulbous nose.   As he slowly
  opens his eyes, I ask him, *Are you Lord Shark*
or shark-man? Could this be an aumakua (ancestral
spirit from Po, the place of shadows) greatest guardian
god of family here to prevent a drowning or kill an enemy?
Or to fish and share the catch? Perhaps, he is here to go swimming
with a shaman. After a time I say, *Show me your teeth!* He slowly opens
mouth and a large jaw protrudes. Then another smaller jaw comes out of first
set of teeth. I nod my head and quietly paddle to the other side of lagoon.

```
        G
         L
          A
           C
            I
             E
w             R                                    n
```
aking up at dusk I go to the patio. Overcast is bright pink as pieces of ice begi
to fall from the sky. It is very scattered this ice.
First the size of buttons. Then alarm clocks,
Shoes, stools, garbage cans, VWs,
2 bedroom cabins . . .
Finally, I decide to
call the authorities.
What's your emergency,
the 911 operator asks.
I'd like to report falling
mini-glaciers
on the commons.
They're light pink
and falling
at the rate
of one per
three minutes
causing slight tremors
and earaches.
Please hold,
she says.
With a steady hand, I immediately pick up my martini.

nocturne

The sky becomes cloudy purple
I see a red disk
Then a larger one
With colored lights in a circle

I ask my friends
Returning from an afternoon
Hike in the woods
If they've seen anything unusual in the sky

They say no
And head back to town

I stay for a few more minutes
To observe a square
In the clouds
Become an abstract painting

Then evolving to another
And another
I think of impressionism
Nouveau art deco

Samba de Orfeu

My flight to Miami
will not leave for another hour
at the invitation of São Paulo's street children
I enter the oblong shelter of bed sheets
and then the adjoining blanket tunnel.

I thank them for their hospitality
think of buying them food
return to a corner *padaria*
but it is closed.
Am I too early or late?

Crossing the street
I buy ten *desayunos jubilosos*   to go
and apologize to *los niños*
for the lack of *pan dulce* .
The taxi starts for the airport:

Now in Miami my friend wants to become mayor
open normal trade relations with *Cuba*.
Says she sees no problems dealing *con El Compañero*.
I give her my support, some ideas, and wish her
success as she drops me off at Miami International.

While disembarking at Chicago's O'Hare
A note handed to me by a stewardess:
Can you sub for me today? One Education class
and one Chicano Culture. Must leave
for Houston today. I e-mail back: Sure!

I visualize *la profesora* taking a side trip
to visit friends in El Paso
then to Mexicali to see her *mamá*.
The map fades and the samba ends.
Another morning through the blinds

Turkey Explodes

Gracious to Gilgamesh
the gobbler is goddamn gone
to godhead nut left to golly gonads
but gobblerdy gook all over da place
Grendal begone greener than greensickness
of Bouncing Betties
wonder giving thanks
or Benny Franklin's birdie

She compared the neck to the penis
not like a guiro or matter
I think only great blue
where are you?
by the Agave River
groggy in fog of servitude
egg and dart
groin compassion

Where is grith?
Grossly I estimate my millage
and eat mazacote
attar of damask may
defeat steel
like cooing cielo
de cilantro
arriba de las conchas.

Then She Kissed El Paco's Lips Now! Or April in DeKalb

The Dreamer

"Help , help,"
        said the throat
                without a mouth.
His leg was where
His arm should have been

Once lifted,   the voice
          returned to its
          reclining position

Hands in his backpockets
   he sighed and said to himself,
                                     "Now what?"

Tony's friend came in and asked,
   "What is happening?"

"Nada," he said.

Then she took the pulse
                of the voice.

Dimension of Poem

Flatness becomes infinity
depth is whiteness blind
surface tension above the words
leaves bottles on these shores
reflecting glints

Then She Kissed El Paco's Lips Now! Or April in DeKalb

A young woman
Leaning against brick wall,
Her hair—undecided blonde or brunette,
Chanting towards Polaris this early afternoon.
Discovers my glance.
Her clubfoot swinging out
Landing straight, she
Wanders in side view mirror,
Eating bagel the wrong way,
On collision course with forever Bum scholar
(Local Legend # 12),
Who has existed on coffee and ciggies
For the last five years,
And for some Hale-Bopp reason,
Is sporting clean-shaven face
With usual backpack.
I hold my breath, driving . . . slowly

Perhaps

April 28, 2001 (Tony and Maureen's wedding day)

Perhaps it was the quote that began
"My husband Tony got to 60 first . . ."
by the Buddhist writer, Darlene, in
Turning Wheel
That started me to think,

Or maybe it was the poets we read, my love,
From your literature book,
The beers I drank, the oles
We ate,
Tomorrow's wedding of a friend,
The Cubs winning in the 8th.

In sleep, one travels.
Near woods by an overpass, I see the
Moon turn
a light blue at dusk.
Clouds like angel hair form small islands on its surface
Then migrate into one land mass,
Break up into continents
A political rainbow of nations
Spinning faster
Like a dial on a slot machine on its side.

The globe becomes yellow orange
And red.
A glowing coal for a star to swallow.

Direk Tutmak

In the dream you pray
spinning like a Dervish
in your shroud

A spiritual birth
at the beginning of creation
Hear the twelve tonalities?

Ecstasy from fusion
of art, music, and dance
the equator: shortest path to God

The eye of certainty is the Divine
between knowledge and truth
"The whole cosmos is a dancing mystery,"
the mystic says.

Why do I love you?

On obsidian-sand
you are opulent opal
my source

You Heard a Robin!

Where were you when this Robin sang?
In the shower? Could this mimic tune
of mocking bird be his memory of another
spring?

Or was it the Box Elder Bug, corner
ventriloquist with dummy under wing?

Were you in the kitchen as rain hit window
and Ladybug Siren on lip of juice glass wailed
telepathically," Where is my sunshine?"

Wait for Vernal Equinox, youth
of celestial time and sphere,
to touch the cool moist tulips, violets,
arboreal buds.

Tomorrow let us sleep an extra
hour in each other's arms
and share a dream of grass, summer breeze,
the flight of worm
in robin's beak.

EPILOGUE

Rezo Resbaloso: Slippery Prayer or Prayer While Sliding

Rezo Resbaloso

How do I pray?
Let me count one way:

Why is salt truck pulling over? Last week all salt trucks going in other direction. Too much ice and snow on the blades? Hit fast selector, amigo. Pulling off. ¿Por qué? Not your territory? Point of your no return? Coward.

My windshield also thanks you for sal, Bladerunner.

Not too tight, pendejo. Firm but suavecito. Float like a mariposa and front-rudder like Capitan Dickweed on choppy Miss. That's funny. No sabía que leather guantes could sweat on the outside, pachuco. Where did that pinche pick-up go to? Visibility mal para patos woo. Crosswind slush sailor soon to be pedo if I reach Santa Nevada en La Hora de Alegría, Ojalá Great Ojalá! Aquí vamos San Pancho Riata en mi pyjamas. Rezo that the first car that goes off the road is not mine. Thirty segundos later a red mustang just spun out. Teenage Mensos Postotes. Cincuenta millas por hora, Vatos Locos, no mas. Rezo otra vez that the segundo carrito que besa la zanja is not mine, por favor.

Ooo Eee Satanás get off of my car fender. Ooo Eee Satanás get off of my car fender. Past the snowy and sleepy pueblo of Seenomore my mueble slides to crooked stop signs y luzes. Not diez minutos pass y otros muchachos, hijos de los arroyos, find casa. But un chota in front. An officer lugarteniente, one of DeeCalbs más finos right there in front of me, ready to assist the slippery slope bandidos. Probably college kids. I put my flashers on and smile at the placa who is not very happy, no señor. ¿Mucho wind, sleet, rain, and snow, Officer Krumpky? Mañana is a better day, no? Rezo one more tiempo. Solamente tres millas. Y nada happens, almost.

Éste es el corrido del suplicante que llego a casa.

Author's Notes

Born and raised in Sterling, Illinois, Ric Amézquita enlisted in the U.S. Air Force in 1966, and served as a sergeant/survival instructor until 1970. After completing his tour, he enrolled as a full-time student at Sauk Valley Community College in Dixon, Illinois, and eventually earned his B.A. and M.A. in Comparative Literature from Sangamon State University (now the University of Illinois at Springfield).

Amézquita applied himself to a wide variety of occupations over the years: He has worked as an adjunct instructor, teaching English Composition, Rhetoric, and Literature, English as a Second Language, courses in nonnative literacy, poetry, and Latin American Culture at various Illinois community colleges and universities. He has also served as a translator for Lutheran Social Services, as a legal advocate and instructor for the Illinois Migrant Council in Rochelle, Illinois, and as an academic counselor in Northern Illinois University's athletic and Latino programs. He recently worked as a contracting specialist for the U.S. Department of Veteran Affairs, National Acquisition Center.

His publications include a chapbook, *Eating Stones* and an electronic book, *Rezo Resbaloso: A Collection of Poems*, Alexander Street Press. His poems have been published in *Discourse: Journal for Theoretical Studies in Media and Culture, Caracol, Revista Chicano-Riqueña, Alchemist Review, Many Smokes, Rockford Review, Spoon River Quarterly*, the first anthology of Mexican American writings about the U.S. war in Southeast Asia Aztlán and Viet Nam: *Chicano and Chicana Experiences of the War*, and other venues. He continues to write poetry, is an active member of one of DeKalb's local poetry workshop groups, and is often invited to read his poetry at local community and university gatherings. He has been a featured guest poet at assorted area coffee houses, bookstores, and has taped readings for local TV.

Books by Pearn and Associates, Inc.

Nonfiction

Love is like a Lizard, Dr. Jerry Gibson, (personal memoir) paper
A Lenten Journey Toward Christian Maturity, William E. Breslin
    (prayer guide, also available in Spanish) paper
Black 14: The Rise, Fall and Rebirth of Wyoming Football, Ryan Thorburn
    (sports biography) paper
*Cowboy Up: Kenny Sailors, The Jump Shot and Wyoming's Championship
    Basketball History,* Ryan Thorburn, (sports biography) paper †*
Dream Season, My Brother Gary and the 1957 Ashland Panthers, Victor W. Pearn
    (sports biography) Kindle Books only*
Goulash and Picking Pickles, Louise Mae Hoffmann (autobiography) cloth & paper
Ikaria: A Love Odyssey on a Greek Island, Anita Sullivan (autobiography) paper*
I Look Around for my Life, John Knoepfle (autobiography) cloth*
It Started & Ended: The Story About a Soldier and Civilian Life, Bud Grounds
    (autobiography) paper
Lost Cowboys: The Bud Daniel Story, and Wyoming Baseball, Ryan Thorburn
    (sports biography) paper
The Great Adventure—Untold, Charles Hamman, cloth & paper*

Novels

Halfway to Eternity, Michael Scott Stevens, (fiction) paper
1945, Joseph J. Kozma, (fiction), paper*
Another Chance, Joe Naiman, (fiction — publisher only) cloth
Light Across the Alley: The Story of a Young Matchmaker, Victor W. Pearn
    (fiction) Kindle Books only*
Point Guard, Victor Pearn (fiction) cloth

Poetry

Then She Kissed El Paco's Lips Now! Or April in DeKalb
    Ricardo Mario Amézquita, paper
Mathematics in Color, Joseph J. Kozma, paper
The Dreamer and the Dream, Rick E. Roberts, paper
Until We Meet, Joseph J. Kozma, paper
walking in snow, John Knoepfle, paper
Shadows and Starlight, John Knoepfle, paper
Apricot Harvest, Victor W. Pearn, paper

Available on Barnesandnoble.com

† Available on Nook; *Available on Kindle Books, Amazon.com. Also available from Ingram Books, and Baker and Taylor. You may order at your local bookstore or directly from the publisher, **victorpearn@ymail.com.**

www.ingramcontent.com/pod-product-compliance
Lightning Source LLC
Chambersburg PA
CBHW022107160426
43198CB00008B/389